Get Ready

Workbook

1

KB067044

Author
LLS English Research Center

Good work!

Good morning

Fabulous!

J PLUS
Language Publishing Co.

Unit 1 — Hello, Alice

Write down the answers.

 Tina

My name is _____ .

 Max

My name is _____ .

 Scott

My name is _____ .

 Bob

My name is _____ .

My name is Alice. What's your name?

Write the answer.

What's your name?

_____

Circle each partner letter.

R   r   t   y

D   a   d   b

N   m   n   h

Q   p   b   q

T   y   t   k

H   h   n   u

E   a   e   o

J   i   l   j

Fill in the blanks.

Aa	Bb	Cc		Ee	
Gg		Ii	Jj		Ll
	Nn	Oo	Pp		
Rr	Ss			Vv	
Xx		Zz

This Is Bob

⁂ **Trace the sentence and say it aloud.**

✓ **Match.**

Good morning.   •   • That's OK.

Nice to meet you. •   • Nice to meet you, too.

I am sorry.   •   • Good morning.

❀ Fill in the blanks.

___ird

___at

___pple

🌀 Circle the beginning letters.

    a   b   c

    a   b   c

    a   b   c

   a   b   c

    a   b   c

    a   b   c

    a   b   c

    a   b   c

    a   b   c

    a   b   c

What's This?

Trace and match.

hamster   cow   goat   bird   dog   cat   duck

Write the answers.

What is this?

It's _____ .

What is this?

_____ .

❀ **Fill in the blanks.**

___oll   ___ish   ___lephant

🌀 **Circle the pairs that have the same beginning sound.**

◣ **Write the beginning letters.**

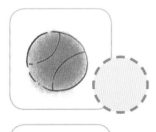

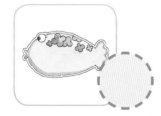

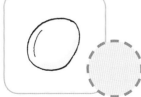

Is It A School Bag?

Write the words.

> pencil   crayon   ruler   chair   school bag   pencil case

_____

_____

_____

_____

_____

_____

Write the answers.

   Is it a chair?

_____ .

   Is it a ruler?

_____ .

Translate into English.

그것은 강아지입니까?

> Is   dog   it   a   ?

_____

Fill in the blanks.

___gloo   ___irl   ___ouse

Choose one in row that has the different beginning sound.

Write the beginning letters.

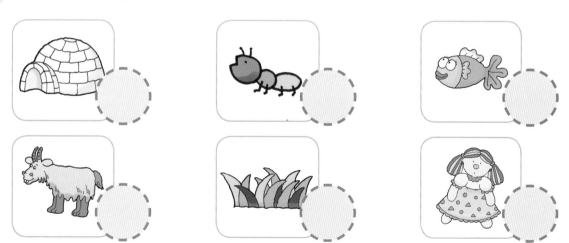

She Is My Sister

🍀 **Fill in the blanks.**

s __ st __ __

__ a __ __ er

gr __ ndm __ t __ er

__ ra __ d __ athe __

b __ o __ her

m __ th __ __

✔ **Read and match.**

Who is she? •

Who is he? •

Who are they? •

• He is my brother.

• They are my mom and dad.

• She is my sister.

◎ **Translate into English.**

이 분은 우리 할머니입니다.

is   grandmother   This   my   .

_____

✤ Fill in the blanks.

___uice   ___ion   ___ite

🌀 Choose all that have the same beginning sound.

Jj

Ll

Kk

◣ Write the beginning letters.

Unit 6 — It's A Star

Read and draw.

square

circle

star

triangle

rectangle

Look at the pictures and fill in the blanks.

What do you have?

I have a _____ .

I have a _____ .

I have a _____ .

Translate into English.

하늘을 봐!

at　sky　the　Look　!

_____

Fill in the blanks.

___ctopus ___ail ___ilk

Match the pictures that have the same beginning sound.

Write the beginning letters.

Write down the words.

three   one   ten
eight   five   four   two
seven   nine   six

_____

_____   _____   _____   _____

_____   _____   _____   _____

Match.

How old are you?   •   • Thank you.

It is for you.   •   • I am 10 years old.

Are you 8 years old?   •   • Yes, I am.

Translate into English.

나는 아홉살이야.

nine   am   I   years   old   .

_____

Fill in the blanks.

___uestion

___ie

___abbit

Choose the correct beginning sound.

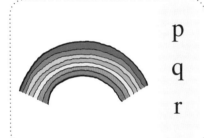
p
q
r

p
q
r

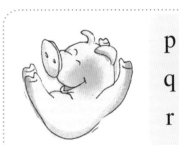
p
q
r

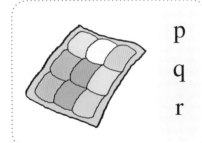
p
q
r

p
q
r

p
q
r

Write the beginning letters.

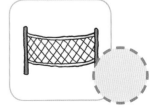

Unit 8 · I Like Pink

Trace and color the balloons.

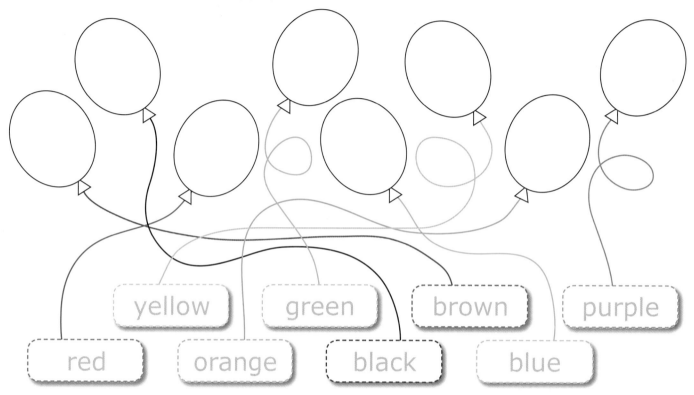

yellow　green　brown　purple

red　orange　black　blue

✓ **Write the correct answers.**

Do you like yellow?

Yes, _____　No, _____

What is your favorite color?

_____

I don't.
I like red.
I do.

◎ **Translate into English.**

나는 보라색을 좋아해.

I　purple　like　.

_____

Fill in the blanks.

___un

___en

___mbrella

Do they both begin with the same sound? Mark O or X.

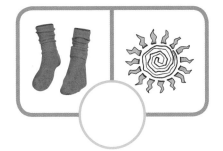

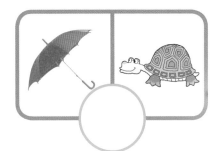

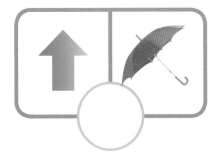

Write the beginning letters.

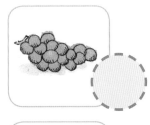

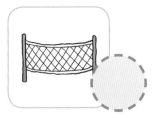

She Is Wearing A Yellow Hat

Trace and match.

pants •

dress •

jacket •

socks •

Read, draw, and then color.

Hi! I am Bob!
I like blue and yellow.
Today I am wearing
blue pants and a
yellow T-shirt.
How do I look?

Translate into English.

그녀는 빨간 치마를 입고 있어.

skirt   wearing   She   is   red   a   .

_____

Fill in the blanks.

___est

___itch

___-ray

Look and write all that have the same beginning sound with given picture.

| watch   van   X-ray   vest   witch   vet   wagon |

_____ _____ _____

_____

_____ _____ _____

Write the beginning letters.

Do a puzzle.

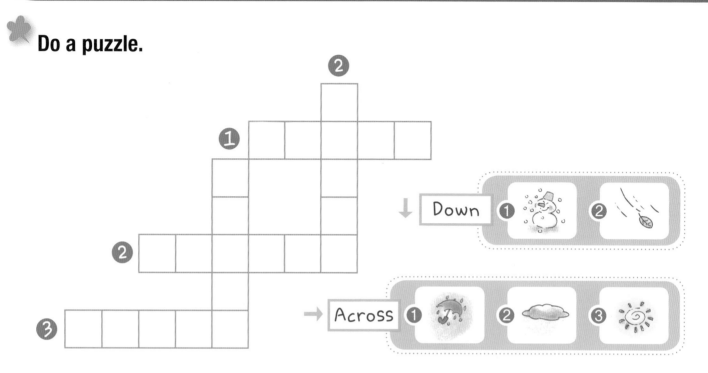

Write the answers.

> It   No,   rainy   is   isn't   it

How is the weather today?

_____ .

Is it sunny?

_____ .

Translate into English.

축구 하러 가자.

> play   Let's   soccer   .

_____

Fill in the blanks.

___oo   ___o-yo   ___ogurt   ___ebra

 Connect the pictures that have the same beginning sound.

 Write the beginning letters.

A Monkey Is On The Tree

Decode.

b	d	e	h	i	n	o	r	t	u	x

_____ _____ _____ _____ _____ _____

_____ _____ _____ _____ _____

Trace and match.

The monkey is under the tree. •

The monkey is in the tree. •

The monkey is next to the tree. •

Translate into English.

원숭이는 나무 뒤에 있어.

> behind   The monkey   is   the tree   .

_____

Fill in the blanks.

h___t   d___g   c___t   r___ck

Read and match.

The cat has a bag.   •   •

The cat has a hat.   •   •

The dog jumps.   •   •

The dog jumps on the rock. •   •

Write the beginning letters.

Unit 12 I Want Some Pizza

Fill in the blanks.

w __ te __

j __ __ ce

ha __ b __ rg __ __

br __ __ d

s __ l __ d

sand __ __ c __

Write the answers.

pizza

What do you want?

_____ _____ _____ _____ .

soda

Do you want some milk?

_____ _____ _____ .

I
No,
want
don't
some

◎ **Translate into English.**

나는 핫도그를 원해.

want   I   a   hotdog   .

_____

Fill in the blanks.

r___d   h___t   b___g   b___g   b___s

Circle the correct vowels.

b__ll

e
i
u

b__g

u
i
e

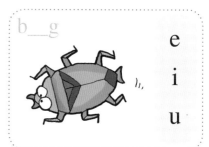
b__g

e
i
u

b__s

e
i
u

h__t

u
i
e

p__t

e
i
u

Draw a line to match from each picture to the correct vowel.

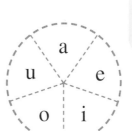

a
u   e
o   i

Let's Play On The Slide

🦋 **Follow the paths and trace the words.**

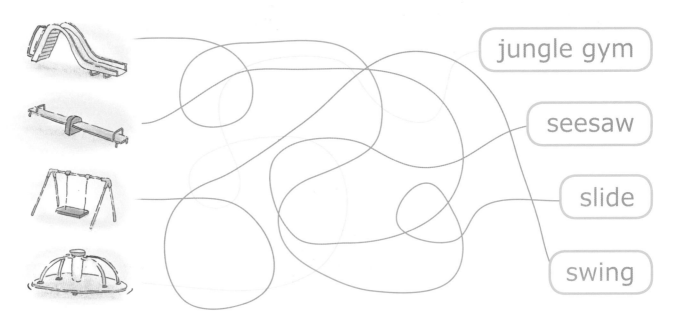

jungle gym

seesaw

slide

swing

✓ **Complete the sentences.**

slide

Let's [ ] on the [ ] .

soccer

[ ] play [ ] .

◎ **Translate into English.**

그네 타자!

play   on   Let's   the   swing   !

_____

Fill in the blanks.

__ __ock

__ __ag

__ __ack

Complete the sentences.

The __ __ock is in the __ __assroom.

It's a __ __ue __ __ute.

I see a __ __ack __ __ag.

Write the beginning letters to complete the words.

I Am A Teacher

Circle the words and check(✓) in the boxes.

F	A	R	M	E	R	L	A	S	T	I	O	W	K
I	Q	U	R	T	M	I	O	S	A	P	E	I	S
R	R	K	C	H	R	T	I	S	O	I	D	E	D
E	T	H	N	W	E	T	H	E	R	L	G	R	A
	Y	B	M	U	T	H	I	T	N	O	C	X	E
F	U	N	U	L	R	A	B	E	K	T	F	D	R
I	I	N	E	O	H	S	U	A	X	Z	P	O	T
G	O	M	E	V	A	K	E	C	U	W	O	C	H
H	E	F	N	E	T	J	C	H	I	D	E	T	G
T	D	H	S	A	G	H	E	E	S	B	V	O	C
E	F	T	A	X	I		D	R	I	V	E	R	V
R	G	W	A	S	T	I	P	J	K	F	G	D	E
P	O	L	I	C	E		O	F	F	I	C	E	R

- teacher ☐
- fire fighter ☐
- farmer ☐
- doctor ☐
- nurse ☐
- police officer ☐
- pilot ☐
- taxi driver ☐

Match and trace the sentences.

- I am a farmer.

- I am a doctor.

- I am a police officer.

Translate into English.

나는 소방관이야.

am   a   fire fighter   I   .

_____

Fill in the blanks.

__ __ass   __ __ide   __ __ant

Circle the correct blends.

   The   pl / gl   ass is small.

   Water the   sl / pl   ant.

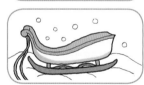   The   sl / cl   ed is in the snow.

Write the correct blends.

__ __ass   __ __ane   __ __ove   __ __ock

__ __ide   __ __ack   __ __ute   __ __ed

The Duck Has Two Legs

Match.

ear

nose

neck

foot

finger

shoulder

head

arm

mouth

eye

leg

hand

toe

Write the answers.

I have ___ legs.

I have ___ eyes.

I have ___ arms.

Translate into English.

나의 개구리는 한 개의 입과 네 개의 발을 가지고 있어.

frog	My	one
legs	mouth	has
four	and	.

_____

🍀 Fill in the blanks.

__ __own

__ __other

__ __ess

🌀 Write the correct blends.

My sister has a __ __own __ __ess.

My __ __other has a __ __um.

The __ __ab has a __ __own.

🔺 Circle the correct blends.

cr
cl

br
pl

gl
dr

cr
cl

fl
bl

br
dr

She Is Clapping

✿ **Write down the meaning of the word.**

Word	fly	sing	jump	eat
meaning	날다			

run	cry	laugh	clap	dance

✓ **Write the answers.**

laugh

What are you doing?

I am _____ .

clap

What are you doing?

_____ .

sing

What are you doing?

_____ .

◎ **Translate into English.**

나는 노래하며 춤추고 있는 중이야.

| and | dancing | I |
| singing | am | . |

_____

Fill in the blanks.

__ __og

__ __ain

__ __ass

Fill in the blanks.

The _____ is on the _____ .

The _____ has some _____ .

fruit
frog
grass

Fill in the blanks.

__ __ack

__ __uck

__ __ock

__ __ass

__ __ane

__ __ant

__ __ag

__ __uit

__ __um

__ __own

Answers

Unit 1

Page 2
My name is Tina. / My name is Max.
My name is Scott. / My name is Bob.

My name is (자신의 이름).

Page 3

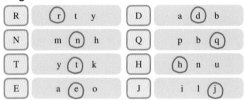

Dd Ff / Hh Kk / Mm Qq / Tt Uu Ww / Yy

Unit 2

Page 4
Good morning.   That's OK.
Nice to meet you.   Nice to meet you, too.
I am sorry.   Good morning.

Page 5
bird cat apple

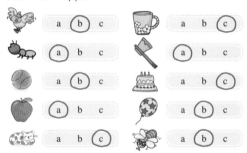

Unit 3

Page 6

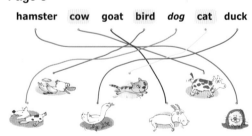

It's a goat.
It's a hamster.

Page 7
doll fish elephant

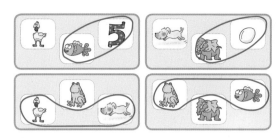

b f c / e a d

Unit 4

Page 8
pencil   ruler
school bag   chair
crayon   pencil case

Yes, it is / Yes, it is

Is it a dog?

Page 9
igloo girl house

i a f / g g d

Unit 5

Page 10
sister   father   grandmother
grandfather   brother   mother

Who is she?   He is my brother.
Who is he?   They are my mom and dad.
Who are they?   She is my sister.

This is my grandmother.

Page 11
juice   lion   kite

k g b / d j i

Unit 6

Page 12

square   circle   star   triangle   rectangle

I have a triangle. / I have a star. / I have a rectangle.

Look at the sky!

Page 13
octopus nail milk

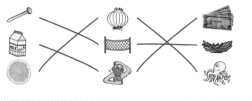

a	n	k	o	c	j
g	h	k	b	m	f

Unit 7

Page 14
one two three four five six seven eight nine ten

How old are you?   Thank you.
It is for you.   I am 10 years old.
Are you 8 years old? —— Yes, I am.

I am nine years old.

Page 15
question pie rabbit

r p p / q r q

e l q g / f k o n

Unit 8

Page 16

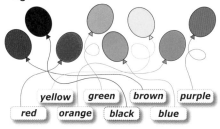

yellow green brown purple
red orange black blue

Yes, I do. No, I don't. / I like red.

I like purple.

Page 17
sun ten umbrella

OXO / OOX

g i j r / n o g n

Unit 9

Page 18

pants
dress
jacket
socks

She is wearing a red skirt.

Page 19
vest witch x-ray

van vest vet / X-ray / watch witch wagon

u m k g / f t e a

Unit 10

Page 20

It is rainy. / No, it isn't.

Let's play soccer.

Page 20
zoo yo-yo yogurt zebra

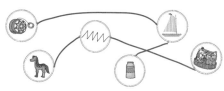

c	l	o	x	h	u
v	i	k	n	w	p

Unit 11

Page 22
behind in on / under next to

The monkey is **under** the tree.
The monkey is **in** the tree.
The monkey is **next** to the tree.

The monkey is behind the tree.

Page 23
hat dog cat rock

Answers

The cat has a bag.
The cat has a hat.
The dog jumps.
The dog jumps on the rock.

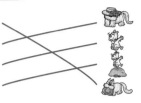

d   c   j   /   h   r   b

Unit 12

Page 24
water   juice   hamburger   /   bread   salad   sandwich

I want some pizza.   /   No, I don't.

I want a hotdog.

Page 25
red   hit   big   bug   bus

bell   big   bug   /   bus   hit   pet

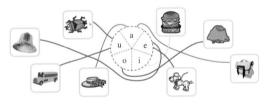

Unit 13

Page 26
Let's play on the slide.   /   Let's play soccer.

Let's play on the swing!

Page 27
clock   flag   black

The clock is in the classroom.
It's a blue flute.
I see a black flag.

class   flute   black   clock   flag

Unit 14

Page 28

F	A	R	M	E	R	L	A	S	T	I	O	W	K
I	Q	U	R	T	M	I	O	S	A	P	E	I	S
R	R	K	C	H	R	T	I	S	O	I	D	E	D
E	T	H	N	W	E	T	H	E	R	L	G	R	A
Y	B	M	U	T	H	I	T	N	O	C	X	E	
F	U	N	U	L	R	A	B	E	K	T	F	D	R
I	I	N	E	O	H	S	U	A	X	Z	P	O	T
G	O	M	E	V	A	K	E	C	U	W	O	C	H
H	E	F	N	E	T	J	C	H	I	D	E	T	G
T	D	H	S	A	G	H	E	E	S	B	V	O	C
E	F	T	A	X	I	D	R	I	V	E	R	V	
R	G	W	A	S	T	I	P	J	K	F	G	D	E
P	O	L	I	C	E	O	F	F	I	C	E	R	

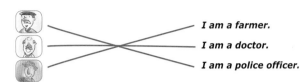

I am a farmer.
I am a doctor.
I am a police officer.

I am a fire fighter.

Page 29
glass   slide   plant

The glass is small.   /   Water the plant.   /   The sled is in the snow.

glass   plane   glove   clock   /   slide   black   flute   sled

Unit 15

Page 30

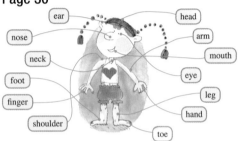

I have five legs.   /   I have two eyes.   /   I have three arms.

My frog has one mouth and four legs.

Page 31
crown   brother   dress

My sister has a brown dress.
My brother has a drum.
The crab has a crown.

cr   pl   gl   /   cl   fl   dr

Unit 16

Page 32

Word	fly	sing	jump	eat
meaning	날다	노래하다	점프하다	먹다
run	cry	laugh	clap	dance
뛰다	울다	웃다	손뼉치다	춤추다

laughing.   /   I am clapping.   /   I am singing.

I am singing and dancing.

Page 33
frog   train   grass

The frog is on the grass.   /   The frog has some fruit.

black   truck   clock   glass   plane
plant   flag   fruit   drum   crown